HOW TO USE THIS NOTEBOOK

SQ3R METHOD

What is SQ3R?

SQ3R (also known as SQRRR) is a reading method recommended for absorbing information from literature such as journal papers, articles and books. It's a particular good tool for essay writing as it supports the reader in first, developing a greater understanding of the literature, before then aiding in the memorization of the information and then finally writing the information in your own words and developing questions for further investigation. These last two steps are key to conducting a productive yet efficient literature search for essay writing.

What does it stand for?

SQRRR stands for Skim, Question, Read, Recall and Review; 'Skim', sometimes replaced with 'Survey', is referring to the process of reading over the details of the chosen to text to get a sense of its suitability, 'Question' is the practice of writing down the questions you need to ask whilst reading the text, 'Reading' means to actively read the text whilst answering your questions, 'Recall' is to recall the main points in your own words and 'Review' is to make sure you've understood the text completely.

Essay Title	
Reference	

Continued from Page		Continued on Page	

SKIM

Make a note of headings, sub-headings and features, such as figures, tables and summary paragraphs. Time: 3-5 minutes.

QUESTION

List your important questions. These can be about the reading in general if you are revising this text or about the information you want to extract from the text if you are writing an essay.

READ

Read actively with the aim of answering the questions you asked on the previous page.

Keeping your questions in mind, read through the text, answering each question as you go.

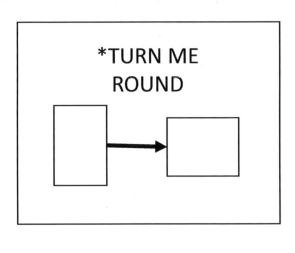

*TURN ME ROUND

Create a mind map of the main points of the text and the answers to your questions from memory.

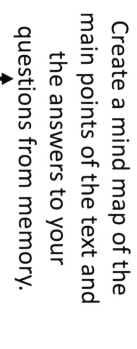

RECALL

If you are revising this will help you to take in the information in the text.

If you are writing an essay or article this will translate the text into your own words.

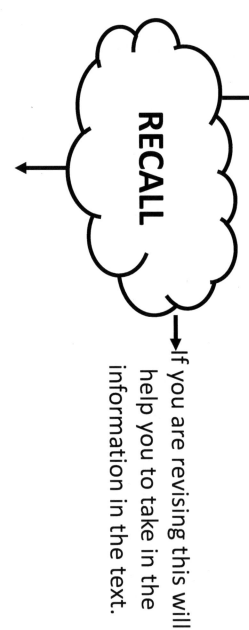

6

Read over the text again and make notes of anything you missed in your original reading. Expand your notes and add more detail.

Also note any questions which need more research to answer. For example;
- Is key information missing?
- Has the text pointed you towards any other references?
- What do you need to do next?

SQ3R
Notes

Essay Title	
Reference	

Continued from Page		Continued on Page	

SKIM

QUESTION

READ

REVIEW

Essay Title	
Reference	

Continued from Page		Continued on Page	

SKIM

QUESTION

READ

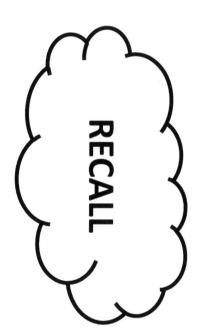

REVIEW

Essay Title	
Reference	

Continued from Page		Continued on Page	

SKIM

QUESTION

19

READ

REVIEW

Essay Title	
Reference	
Continued from Page		Continued on Page	

SKIM

QUESTION

READ

REVIEW

Essay Title	
Reference	
Continued from Page		**Continued on Page**	

SKIM

QUESTION

READ

REVIEW

Essay Title	
Reference	

Continued from Page		Continued on Page	

SKIM

QUESTION

READ

REVIEW

Essay Title	
Reference	

Continued from Page		Continued on Page	

SKIM

QUESTION

READ

REVIEW

Essay Title	
Reference	

Continued from Page		Continued on Page	

SKIM

QUESTION

READ

REVIEW

Essay Title	
Reference	

Continued from Page		Continued on Page	

SKIM

QUESTION

READ

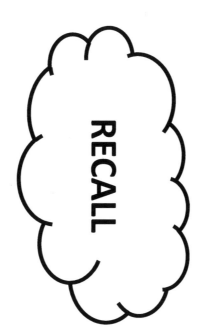

REVIEW

Essay Title	
Reference	

Continued from Page		Continued on Page	

SKIM

QUESTION

READ

REVIEW

Essay Title			
Reference			
Continued from Page		**Continued on Page**	

SKIM

QUESTION

READ

RECALL

REVIEW

Essay Title	
Reference	

Continued from Page		Continued on Page	

SKIM

QUESTION

READ

REVIEW

Essay Title	
Reference	
Continued from Page	

		Continued on Page	

SKIM

QUESTION

READD

READ

REVIEW

Essay Title	
Reference	

Continued from Page		Continued on Page	

SKIM

QUESTION

READ

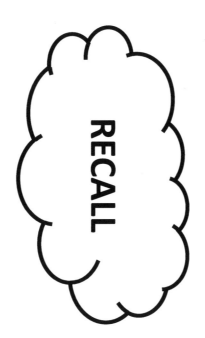

REVIEW

Essay Title	
Reference	

Continued from Page		Continued on Page	

SKIM

QUESTION

READ

REVIEW

Essay Title	
Reference	

Continued from Page		Continued on Page	

SKIM

QUESTION

READ

Essay Title	
Reference	

Continued from Page		Continued on Page	

SKIM

QUESTION

READ

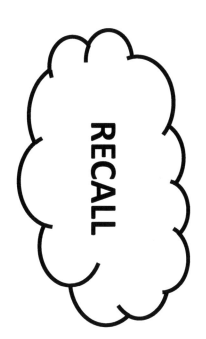

REVIEW

Essay Title	
Reference	
Continued from Page	Continued on Page

SKIM

QUESTION

READ

REVIEW

Essay Title	
Reference	

Continued from Page		Continued on Page	

SKIM

QUESTION

READ

RECALL

REVIEW

Essay Title	
Reference	
Continued from Page		**Continued on Page**	

SKIM

QUESTION

READ

REVIEW

Essay Title	
Reference	

Continued from Page		Continued on Page	

SKIM

QUESTION

READ

REVIEW

Essay Title	
Reference	

Continued from Page		Continued on Page	

SKIM

QUESTION

READ

REVIEW

Essay Title	
Reference	

Continued from Page		Continued on Page	

SKIM

QUESTION

RECALL

REVIEW

Essay Title	
Reference	

Continued from Page		Continued on Page	

SKIM

QUESTION

READ

REVIEW

Essay Title	
Reference	

Continued from Page		Continued on Page	

SKIM

QUESTION

READ

Made in the USA
Las Vegas, NV
27 November 2024